FOLKTALES AND LEGENDS OF NORFOLK

By
G. M. DIXON
And illustrated by
MALCOLM WALKER

Minimax Books

ISBN 0 906791 10 3

© MINIMAX BOOKS LTD. 1980
Deeping St. James, Peterborough
Second Edition 1983

Printed in England by

FORUM·PRINT Ltd.

CONTENTS

The Headless Horseman   Page 5
The Cube Church   Page 8
The Green Man of Norwich   Page 12
Boadicea   Page 16
The Potter Heigham Drummer   Page 19
The Burning of King's Lynn Witch   Page 22
Black Shuck   Page 25
Murder at Stanfield Hall   Page 28
Wickhampton Hearts   Page 31
Happisburgh Smuggler   Page 35
Walsingham Shrine   Page 38
Old Door Handle   Page 41
Pedlar of Swaffham   Page 45
Bawburgh Wells   Page 48
Legend of the Shrieking Pit   Page 51
St. Edmund   Page 54
Babes in the Wood   Page 58
Amy Robsart   Page 61

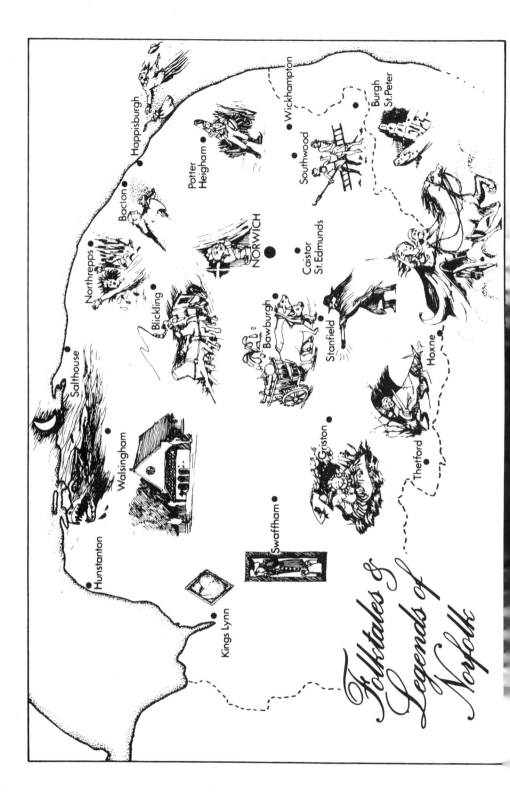

Folktales &
Legends of
Norfolk

Happisburgh
Bacton
Potter Heigham
Wickhampton
Burgh St. Peter
Southwood
Northrepps
NORWICH
Caistor St. Edmunds
Blicking
Salthouse
Bawburgh
Stanfield
Hoxne
Walsingham
Griston
Thetford
Hunstanton
Swaffham
Kings Lynn

THE HEADLESS HORSEMAN

Stories of headless horsemen, presagers of death, have their origin in the beautiful mansion at Blickling near Aylsham. It is now owned by the National Trust, having been donated to them by the Marquis of Lothian. Visit it now on a summer day and the dark days of Blickling will seem a mere blink away.

When Henry VIII executed Anne Boleyn, that troubled man had bigger worries on his mind than the fate of the father, Sir Thomas Boleyn, who resided at Blickling Hall. Denied a son by Catherine of Aragon, who bore him only Mary, destined to be the unpopular Mary I, Henry VIII turned his affections to Anne Boleyn and found in her a ready and worthy accomplice. Henry, in keeping with the times, could have kept her as a mistress, but, like all monarchs of that era, wanted a legitimate son to succeed him. Therefore he needed to marry Anne and have an acknowledged honourable successor to the throne.

Thus he courted her and, with his counsellors, devised ways of breaking his marriage to Catherine. As history tells us, the Church would not sanction divorce, and he had to break with the Roman Church in order to rid himself of Catherine in favour of the lady in waiting, Anne Boleyn. Sir Thomas Boleyn was delighted when his beautiful daughter was originally accepted as a lady in waiting to Catherine. Proud was his step around the estates of Blickling as he boasted of his daughter's preferment at the lively and prestigious court of King Henry VIII. When he saw that his daughter had caught the favourable eye of the King, Sir Thomas's pride knew no bounds for the designation of mistress had no stigma attached to it. Sir Thomas was proud of his daughter and spoke with the King and told him that he was pleased that his daughter was in receipt of the King's favour. But, already, the web was being woven that would ultimately doom Sir Thomas to his penance. When Catherine was divorced and Anne married the King, Sir Thomas's delight knew no bounds. When Anne was with child Sir Thomas was a favoured visitor at court, and on his lands at Blickling the proud father of the Queen of England strode down the gravelled walks of Blicking Hall with irresistible vigour. We, who know the story, know the fate of the mother but her father had not the eye of history as we have; his fate was closer. When a daughter was born, Sir Thomas foresaw her fate, but even he could not predict the callousness of Henry VIII when he put Anne to death on a trumped up charge of treachery.

When Anne was executed on 19th May, 1536, the picture of her death would not leave Sir Thomas. He could not bear to attend the execution but someone told him of how Anne gently smiled at the gentleman who brought her from the tower, saying "I hear the executioner is very skilful; my neck is very small."

Sir Thomas fled to his Blickling estate and hid in the Hall, a sadly deflated man. The horrors of the death which his beautiful and beloved daughter had met haunted him and he was obsessed by the thought of the head being severed from the body.

His mind continually played with this thought and when he died six years later it was still uppermost in his half crazed mind. "For that cruel death" he vowed, "I will lose my head, and the country will know it. For the eleven years she was with me are eleven bridges to my happiness and I will cross them for a thousand years to regain that pleasure and so that my soul may rest."

And so Sir Thomas died, tormented by his daughter's death and by his aiding and abetting of the marriage.

On May 19th, for a thousand years, the headless ghost of Sir Thomas, driving a coach pulled by four headless horses, crosses the eleven bridges at Aylsham, Burgh, Oxnead, Buxton, Hautbois, Coltishall, Belaugh, the two Meyton bridges, and Wroxham, in an attempt to atone for the death of his daughter.

6

As he rides the roads and crosses the bridges he calls to any passerby, and it is a certainty that if the passerby shows that he hears the ghost of Sir Thomas he will be carried off to purgatory. 'Tis best to pretend you do not hear.

THE CUBE CHURCH

The river folk who ply the holiday waters by Beccles often have their attention caught by the sight of the curious church tower at Burgh St. Peter, some two miles from the village. It has the appearance of a tower of toy bricks, getting smaller and smaller, which have been piled up by a child. Attached to this is the thatched body of the church, one hundred feet long and fourteen feet wide. The visitors scratch their heads in wonderment and the more discerning ones see the fragments of the old priory in the field close by and some Roman tiles set in the church wall. All very puzzling, but they can thank their lucky stars they are not ther on May 2nd.

Adam Morland owned a poor farm in Burgh St. Peter way back in Saxon times. The Roman castle still stood proud and strong at nearby Burgh although it had been ransacked by the Saxons and Angles who had now settled peacefully in the land.

Adam's thatched house, with walls made from wood and mud, stood on a shallow rise on the marshes. He had wrested the land from the marsh and cultivated it with his own hands and some help from his good wife, Martha, and the few oxen he owned. But his wife's face was pinched and of his eight children only three had survived; a fine son, Roger, a daughter, Ann, and a sickly child, Robert, whom Adam did not expect to reach adulthood. Adam turned more and more desperately to his work, attempting to get some kind of living from the windswept, bleak land. He was a gentle and quiet man who loved the marshes and the land, and only wished that he could provide a better and healthier life for his wife and children. He knew that if he could afford better seed and dig better drains his land would produce fivefold his present harvest. But each year at the time of reckoning, by the time he had

gathered together the tithes for the rector and the tribute to the lord of the manor, he had little left to increase his stock and nothing at all after he had provided for his wife and family.

After a harvest which had been ruined by almost incessant rain, Adam was in a sorry situation. He had just enough to pay his dues, but nothing left over to keep his family through the winter. In that bitter winter Martha went down with a fever and only her love for her husband and her love of life enabled her to pull through. Robert, the youngest child, died, and as the spring sun crept over the marshes, Adam wandered about wondering whether to leave his farm and seek his fortune elsewhere.

His wanderings led him by St. John's Priory where he saw the monks going to and fro, happy and singing in their work. One monk listened to Adam's plight but it seemed that he could offer Adam no more assistance than a special prayer. So Adam sat down on a fallen willow trunk and held his head in his hands. He looked up when he heard soft footsteps which paused, and he saw that on the willow beside him there sat an old man. The old man had a tired but kindly voice which encouraged Adam to relate his troubles. Then from his bag the old man drew ten gold coins and pressed them into Adam's hand. Adam protested but the old man said that all he wanted was Adam's thumbprint in a block of wax he carried and repayment in ten years time. Unable to believe his good fortune, Adam gladly pressed his thumb into the wax and promised full repayment. No sooner had he done so, than the old man threw off his cloak and cowl and dashed off up the road. Aghast, Adam saw that the 'old man' had assumed the form of the devil and realised that he had sold his soul to him. He dashed home and told his wife the strange story, which Martha found most difficult to believe, but seeing her husband's sincerity she discussed the matter with him.

As a result of the discussions, Adam used part of the money to improve the farm, but part of it he used to buy the materials to build a small church on the same site as the present one. This he constructed with the help of some friends.

But, the time for repayment came and Adam, now exhausted by his labours on the farm and the church, died three days before the appointed time for him to repay the money or give his soul to the devil.

So, on 2nd May each year an 'old man' haunts the churchyard, his clothes covering nothing but a skeleton with the fires of hell burning inside it. Holidaymakers on that day should just keep going.

THE GREEN MAN

The legend of the Green Man of Norwich is like the green man himself: too indefinite to be called a memory, too factual to be called a superstition. Stand and gaze at the portrayal of him on the Wild Man inn sign in Bedford Street and on the Green Man sign at Rackheath on the main Norwich to Stalham road. His existence is real, his whereabouts unknown.

Once upon a long time ago, Danu, the last of the green men, lived in the woods just to the south east of the present day Norwich. He was small, dressed all in green and had a sharp pointed nose and ears to match. His home was among the trees down by the water, where he knew the quiet trodden ways, the sheltered sunny dells, and the shady pools where the fish were easy to catch. All day he would spend either in his beloved woods, or flitting into the nooks and crannies of Norwich where he gained vast amusement watching the antics of the human folk there. Some people swore that they saw him, but only out of the corners of their eyes; turning to look at him they would find he had vanished. But always there was the flash of that wild face and green suit to remind all the good Norwich folk that Danu was there.

One day he was in King Street, sitting unseen on ledges, peeping from behind a chimney stack, glancing through a door ajar, hidden in the shadowed corner of a wall having a fine time among the merchants' houses there. Suddenly he heard the sound of weeping and, peering over the bedroom window ledge of a fine house, he saw a young girl weeping bitterly. "What shall I do?" the young girl sobbed. "How can I get out of marrying that horrible man?" Unable to contain his curiosity, Danu jumped through the open window and sat on the sill. The young girl was scared and made to hide behind the curtains of her bed, but Danu

12

cried out, "Do not be afraid. Tell me your troubles and let me see if I can help you."

The young girl's sobbing slowly ceased as she looked at Danu and told him her story. She was Alizon, the eldest daughter of Simon Walpole, and she had been promised by her father to marry Philip Crump, a miserly, miserable merchant, twenty years older than herself. This was to win for the father increased riches and a share in Philip Crump's business. "Oh, he is horrible," she sobbed anew, "And I will do anything to get out of it. But my father's mind is made up and there is no escape for me. I have to stay locked in my room until the wedding and that is to be on Saturday. Oh, what can I do?"

Danu thought, as Alizon put her head to her pillow and wept beautiful tears which clung to her dark lashes before trickling down her cheeks.

"Anything?" he asked. "Will you do anything?"

"Anything," she cried. "Yes, I would do anything rather than condemn myself to a life with him."

"Then this is what you must do," continued Danu. "I will come back again on Friday evening at eight o'clock, and if by then you have guessed my name you will go free, and you will not have to marry Philip. But if you have not guessed my name, then you will have to come and live with me."

Alizon looked at Danu and did not know which would be the worse, for that little wild green man would never be a husband to her. But Philip: no, never.

"All right," she said, "I agree."

Danu leapt through the window and although Alizon jumped up straight away she did not see the little figure scampering off into the shadows and across Conisford Bridge.

Calling in her servant Matilda, Alizon breathlessly told her of the encounter with the little green man. Matilda did not know if the forthcoming marriage had deprived Alizon of her senses but she did as she was told and went to John Prior, Alizon's lover, and told him of Alizon's plight.

John did not know where to look nor who to ask. He went in to the inns and hostelries of the city but people laughed at his strange mission and suggested that he go to Babel. Through the streets John wandered all the Wednesday and that Thursday also. By midnight on Thursday he had begun to despair and in his despondency he roamed out of the city and on to the marshes.

Here the last hours of the night were alive with the sounds of the marsh: the scurrying of voles, the rustling of mice, the croaking of frogs, the whirring of owls and the whisk and whine of the breeze as it whispered through the rushes and bushes. John wandered on and on and as the first light hushed over the eastern sky, John saw a light flickering in the trees. His steps took him towards it, and, from his hiding place in the bushes, he saw a little green man dancing around a fire near an oak tree and singing as he danced:

> I will have you
> My lovely girl,
> To be my bride so true.
> I'll give you no clue,
> My lovely girl,
> My name: it just grew and grew.
> Your gamble you will rue,
> My lovely girl,
> For you'll never guess my name, Danu.

John heard, and with mighty relief, and smiling at his good fortune, he retraced his steps to the city. His search had exhausted him and it would be well to gain some sleep before he went to tell Alizon the news.

And so he fell asleep and was aghast, when he woke, to find that it was twenty five minutes to eight. There was half a mile to run before he got to Alizon's house and he ran all the way and summoned the maid, Matilda. She came running and when he told her his story, she quickly wrote the name on a small piece of paper, put it under a glass of wine and went up the stairs to Alizon's room.

Danu was already there, and, hearing the knock on the door, ran behind the curtain. Matilda entered and saw her mistress had been weeping; she smiled as she put down the tray with the glass of wine and pointed to the paper.

When Matilda had gone Danu came round the curtain and taunted Alizon saying that she would never guess his name and that soon she would be in the woods with him.

But Alizon quietly said, "I will keep my promise, and you will keep yours, Danu."

With a shriek of rage, Danu fled and Alizon waited to see what would happen in the morning.

News came at eleven o'clock the next morning that Philip Crump had been killed when an oak tree had fallen on his carriage in Shotesham. This left Alizon free to marry John and they both lived happily ever after, and so did Danu.

BOADICEA

Resistance to conquering invaders has always attracted both admiration and followers. Queen Boadicea has never lacked either, and various places in Norfolk have associations with the lady who led one of the flings of the Ancient Britons against the Romans. History has lent her a noble character which some have tried to belittle, but she lives on, as one of the worthy daughters of Norfolk.

Boadicea had grown up in a tribe where battles were the noble breeding ground of warriors, and in which only the strongest survived be they men or women. This was the Iceni tribe who had their home in Norfolk. Some say that the capital of the tribal lands was at Caistor St. Edmunds, just south of the present day Norwich, where the Romans later built a fort.

When Boadicea was a teenager in 43 A.D. the Iceni were about to be invaded by the Catuvellauni tribe from Essex and they prepared for battle. They were saved when the Romans invaded the Catuvellauni, but their elation was short-lived as the Romans conquered the great Iceni in 47-48 A.D. Prasutagus, the Iceni king, married Boadicea but he turned out to be only a puppet of the Romans and Boadicea longed for her husband's death so that they might be free of the Romans.

When Prasutagus died in 60 A.D., he willed that a half of his kingdom should go to his two daughters, and the other half should be given to the Roman Emperor Nero. But the Romans wanted everything and so they took over the kingdom and possessions of Prasutagus, raping the two daughters and giving Boadicea a public lashing for good measure.

This infuriated the Queen who had been nurtured in the warrior tradition of the Iceni. So much so in fact that she straightaway aroused her tribesmen to revolt.

At this time she was nearly forty, her hair was long, and, according to Roman historians, white. But she was every inch a Queen and she had a remarkable gift of oratory. To the Britons, and the Iceni especially, she was a god-sent gift for they had long hated the cruel rule of the Romans. She soon gathered a force of several thousands and marched for the Roman bases in the south of the country. Omens preceded their advance, for the Channel was said to have flowed red, houses were seen in the Thames, and in Colchester the Roman statue to the god Victory fell flat on its' face.

It was fortunate that the main Roman force was in Anglesey carrying out the final round up and slaughter of the Druids, for Boadicea was able to achieve easy victories at

Colchester, London and St. Albans. In these cities the British revolutionaries were merciless, slaughtering in their thousands the Romans they found and the Britons who had worked either with or for them. Dreadful carnage was reported and, whilst we can deplore it, their exploits excited jubilation among the Britons and there were many recruits anxious to swell the victorious ranks.

Boadicea, the Norfolk Queen of the Iceni, was exultant and, flushed with success, harangued her followers in preparation for the great battle ... the final battle ... the ultimate slaughter of the Romans ... that was soon to take place. Suetonius Paulus, the chief Roman general who had led the Roman Army in its genocide of the Druids, had marshalled his forces somewhere to the north of St. Albans. Here, he arranged his forces in the shape of a wedge with the infantry in the centre and the cavalry on the wings. He counselled his men to keep the wedge firm at all costs.

The appearance of the hordes of Boadicea was a terrible sight both in their numbers and in their ferocity, and so confident was Boadicea of victory that even the women and children from the provision carts had followed the fighting men and gathered like spectators. The savages of Boadicea advanced, yelling and screaming, hurling their weapons and attacking in a frenzy of blood lust and vengeance.

The discipline and training of the Romans held firm however. Relentlessly the Roman wedge moved forward slaying all in its path, and, faced with this invincible slaughter machine, the Britons fled, after thousands had been massacred, women and children among them.

Boadicea and her daughters escaped but rather than face the degradation of inevitable capture, Boadicea poisoned her daughters before committing suicide herself by drinking poison. It is said that her body was brought back to Norfolk by faithful followers and buried at Quidenham under a long low mound about a quarter of a mile from the church.

The Romans then wreaked a terrible revenge on the people of Norfolk for the excessive misdeeds done by Boadicea at Colchester, London and St. Albans. The Norfolk reprisal took generations to·overcome, but by then, the Iceni were no more.

THE POTTER HEIGHAM DRUMMER

Potter Heigham, a large Broadland village, is a place of bridges, water, boats, modern shops, bungalows and marinas. Nestled among this modern tourist development are russet bricked cottages which appear to have always been there, they look so natural. In one of these cottages a young heart once beat, full of pure love and simple passion.

Just over two hundred years ago Potter Heigham was a small village of rich farms for on those flatlands of dark brown soil, crops grew richly and animals thrived on the lush pastures down by the river. Even where the meadow could not be drained and became marsh, men could still wrest a living from the bushes and vegetation which grew in abundance there. The young branches of the willow and alder were cut and stripped for weaving into baskets and the reeds and rushes which could be mown there provided the finest thatching material in the country. Animals, birds and fish, fine for the dinner plate, could be trapped and caught, and living was good, though lean and cold in winter. The men who worked these marshes, living in their cottages on the road bordering the marshes, were a mild, quiet breed, softly spoken and gentle, but as tough and resisting as the lands and material of their trade.

Such a man was Jesse Ducker who lived in Potter Heigham in 1814, a marshman and one of the best. He had a wife Mary at home, the mother of his five children, two sons and three daughters. He loved his children and looked forward to good marriages for his daughters and fine jobs on the marshes for his two sons. The children were all of good stock and the youngest, Jimmy, was the spoilt darling of them all. The eldest son George was a quiet boy who loved the marshes and the birds that flew there in their thousands. Beryl, the youngest daughter, was vain; Eliza, the middle one was of a jealous, quarrelsome nature, but Lilian, at eighteen, the eldest of all the children, was the apple of her father's eye. Soft brown hair, quiet happy eyes and a roundness of face and figure lent her a loveliness and charm that made old men remember the dreams of their youth. One cold February day she went out shopping with her shawl over her head and a warm coat round her, but even these heavy clothes could not hide her charm. As she walked through the village, she saw, resplendent in his uniform, a young soldier home on leave. It was John Sadler of Hickling, whom she had last seen five years ago when they played on the marshes together. John sa·v Lilian with eyes that spoke of Norfolk, home and peace. They fell in love instantly, each of their hearts beating stronger with a warm passion that only young lovers know. They met, and spoke with an assurance and vitality that made the hours vanish in the light of their eyes and the glow of their breasts. Lilian asked John home and he went with her and spent the day close beside her by the fire in the cottage.

But, as dusk whispered over the marshes at half past four, Jesse came home, and when he saw his precious daughter's fascination with the young soldier, he grew harsh and said that his daughter would never marry a soldier. John protested that once the great battle was over in which he was to fight that summer, some said it was to be at Waterloo, he would leave the army and settle down. "Let it be until then," cried Jesse, "but now you will go." John left the house, but not before whispering to Lilian to wait at Swim Coots, a spot close to the edge of Hickling Broad on the Potter Heigham side.

Next evening Lilian waited by the frozen Broad at four o'clock and was thrilled to the shivering marrow of her bones to hear first the roll of the drum and then the swish of skates, as her soldier dramatically came to meet her. They talked and planned and whispered their love for each other before the dark misty night came, and John left, whistling over the ice in the gathering gloom.

Each night she waited, and each night for a week and a day John came, the dashing figure of her dreams and thoughts, to warm her blood on those cold February evenings.

On the ninth night, 24th February, 1814, darkness had come early, but Lilian waited and soon her ears were rewarded by the rolling of the drum as her soldier whistled

over the ice. But, to her cold horror, the drum roll was
suddenly silenced by a terrific creak, a cracking splash …
and silence. She screamed, she waited; she wailed a loud
mourning howl and waited, dementedly treading the marshy
shore. Her soul shivered out over the twitching Broad with
her last wail of anguish before her father, hearing her
torment, came running, and bore his beloved daughter
homewards to a desolation that took her years to overcome.
But, on February nights, at the glooming time, the figure
of a phantom skater can still sometimes be seen, beating a
roll on his drum, as he tries to find the long lost soul of his
love on the Heigham side of Hickling Broad.

THE BURNING OF THE KINGS LYNN WITCH

The Tuesday Market Place at Kings Lynn is alive on that day with stalls and their vendors, and people from the surrounding rural area. In the noise, the chatter, the hum of the cars, and the hurry and the scurry, only the occasional eye sees in the north-west corner of the market place a curious brick. It is diamond shaped and has a heart carved in the centre. Find it and stand and wonder at its strange story.

Margaret Read lived down one of the many small alleys that ran down to the busy quays on the River Ouse. Her small house had crooked windows and a rough door set in its plastered walls and would make the modern house agent drool. The little diamond panes blinked at the narrow street and the glass was somewhat cobwebbed and dusty. Even so, few passersby glanced into the dark interior, and certainly none of the neighbours or those who knew the place did. For in the 1570's and 1580's Margaret, or Shady Meg as she was called, was a feared woman, looked at with awesome dread by the superstitious folk of those days. Margaret Read was a witch.

It was said after her death, when people felt able to talk about her safely, that she had inherited her black powers from her young aunt, Agnes Shipwell, who had died in nearby Grimston at the early age of twenty seven. Margaret had come to Lynn and had set up house there. Firstly she became the confidante of several hags of the poor streets and had, over the years, gained the reputation of being able to make things happen. Her narrow, sharp face and scrawny neck garnished by wispy grey-brown hair excited the first whispers that she had powers that ordinary folk could not use. Soon a small trickle of people with troubles began to frequent her cottage, but nothing could loose their lips to tell of what happened behind the door of Shady Meg's home. Entry to the house was limited and because they did not know, people started to build up the little things that they did see. For instance, why had a large spider made his

22

home unmolested in the corner of Margaret's window? Why was it that a plague of mice had ruined sacks of flour in Mr. Homlit's shop on the corner? Why was it that Mr. Scase's dog had died suddenly, and with no apparent reason? How did Shady Meg get the money to support herself? Why was it that evil smoke came from her chimney at the strangest times and even in the middle of summer? These and other things made the neighbours suspect Shady Meg and she was the centre of continual gossip. People watched her visitors and one of them particularly engaged their attention. This was young Marion Harvey who was pretty and who bore a child. Common tongues wagging, the rumour gained ground that it was Nick Kirk who was responsible and that he had since taken up with another woman. Marion, her face pinched with vengeance, visited Shady Meg late in the evening and after her visits neighbours heard a muttering and calling from the cottage and the street was alive with premonition.

Nick laughed when he heard the rumour, but his laughter was silenced a week later when he felt severe pains in his chest and stomach. Three days later he was dead and his parents immediately suspected the occult powers of Shady Meg.

Soon the voiced suspicions had aroused the authorities who came to Margaret Read's cottage and bore her away screaming and shouting. They searched her house and found a vast, mysterious and dark hoard. Among this clutter was a small figure of a young man with pins thrust through his chest and stomach. According to the custom of the time Margaret was tried by ducking. Taking her to the side of the River Ouse, the soldiers tied her hands and feet and a long line was affixed to her neck. To the ragged cheer of the onlookers Margaret was thrown in and it was seen that she floated for a while and then disappeared beneath the surface, fury on her contorted features and curses emitting from her mouth. The sinking body dragged the line through the hands of those who held it. After what seemed an age, Captain Gotts of the guard gave the order to haul in. The line was pulled in and, coughing and gasping, Shady Meg was hauled out and taken away and locked up.

Because she floated it was coldy decided that Margaret was guilty and she must be burnt to death.

A whispering crowd gathered on the morning of July 20th, 1590, on the Tuesday Market Place, where they saw a pile of faggots around a central stake. Shady Meg, strangely silent, was brought in and tied to the stake. The faggots were fired and a dull flame and swirling smoke hid Shady Meg. The mesmerised onlookers saw occasional glimpses of Margaret wrestling with her bonds, but, as the flames grew higher, she suddenly gave a loud shriek and a loud bang was heard. A missile was seen to fly from the fire and the crowd gasped as they saw that Shady Meg's heart had flown from her body and had struck the wall.

A week later it was noticed that on the very same spot where the heart had hit the wall, a spider had cast a web over a newly fitted brick: a brick that was diamond shaped and had a heart carved in it.

BLACK SHUCK

Stories of the ghost of a large black dog have frightened young and old in North Norfolk for many years. The people along the coast know him as Old Shuck, a name derived from the Anglo Saxon word 'soucca' meaning demon. There are many stories of people seeing the great dog, but only one of the origin of the apparition.

The night of January 28th, 1709, was one of those which was dreaded by the seafarers who sailed their craft through the Devil's Throat, that temperamental stretch of sea off the north easterly corner of Norfolk between Blakeney and Mundesley. Waves, twenty feet high, rose white and murderous, lashed by the howling violence of a gale that tore at the sea and the earth like the screaming destruction of a demon child. The foaming, spuming waves roared across the sea flaying everything in their path before exploding in a rush of water and a buffeting gale blast on the flat seashore. The storm rushed headlong over the marshes to wreak its fury among the trees, houses and churches nestling against the slight rise of land at the edge of the marshes. Trembling hearts within the cottages prayed for God's deliverance whilst others, more hard-headed, anticipated the pickings of a shipwreck.

And shipwreck there was that night on the beach of Salthouse. In the early hours of the morning the brig 'Ever Hopeful' from Whitby had been caught by the storm whilst returning to Yorkshire from London, loaded with a cargo of fruit, spices and other foodstuffs. The captain and crew helplessly tried to manoeuvre their small craft in the screaming wind but, in the darkness, they were carried towards the shallow shoals off the coast which were unlit, save the flickering beacons on the top of the church towers at Cromer and Blakeney. Inevitably, the ship gave a lurch and a tearing sound of timber was heard above the howling wind as she grounded on a bank off Salthouse. The pounding waves hurled their fury on the helpless craft and soon she started to break up, spars, doors and rails being whirled aloft by the dark exulting waves. The screams of the terrified, doomed crew added to the nightmare as they clung to the disintegrating ship or were torn off from the hold. The captain, seeing that to stay would be but to delay death, resolved to make a desperate bid for life. Seizing his pet, a large wolf hound, by the collar, he jumped clear of the ship and was swallowed by the turbulent waves. They struck for the shore only tens of yards away but they were overcome by the currents and roughness of the waters and drowned.

Their bodies were washed ashore and in the quiet morning air the villagers came across them amidst the scattered remnants of the craft, its cargo and crew. Gathering the valuable wood and flotsam together, the men saw the dead

captain still grasping the dog's collar, and the dog's jaws still clamped to the captain's reefer jacket, aptly telling of how man and dog had clung to each other in their desperate attempt for survival. The rest of the crew had perished also. The Salthouse folk discussed the fate of the ship and the crew in hushed whispers as they loosed the captain from his dog. A hole was dug in the sand on the beach and the large wolf hound was buried there, the captain being taken to Salthouse Church where he was buried in an unmarked grave.

Within a few weeks people had seen a large black dog howling and running to seek its master between Cley and Salthouse. As the years have passed his appearance has become more grotesque. He now has large red eyes, is as black as ebony, shaggy and is the size of a calf. People have sensed the hound padding behind them, but a story has never been told of a man who has escaped the jaws of Black Shuck; those people never come back to tell the tale. Apparently he is especially active on those nights around January 28th and whenever the sea is lashed by storms and his terrible howls are borne above the sound of the roaring wind. It would be a foolish person indeed who would scorn the tenacity of Old Shuck and would roam the marshes between Salthouse and Cley at night.

MURDER AT STANFIELD HALL

Stanfield Hall, near the market town of Wymondham, is a beautiful mansion, and the sight of it basking in the calm summer sunshine makes this story seem unreal and fantastic. Yet its truth is well-documented for Stanfield Hall was the scene of two dreadful murders, which resulted in the last public execution in Norwich.

On the evening of November 28th, 1848, James Rush, the tenant of Potash Farm, near Stanfield Hall, had arranged to go to a musical evening in Norwich with Miss Sandford, the governess to his large family of children. James Rush's wife had died six years earlier and Miss Sandford had been hired in London as a governess to his children, subsequently becoming his mistress.

He had had several encounters with the law when he was involved in, among other things, setting fire to a cornstack and harbouring a man who was hiding from the police. Suspicion surrounded the death of his father following a doubtful accident whilst cleaning a gun, and his mother had died a short time after consuming food and drink prepared and given to her by James.

Monies inherited from his parents enabled James to hire farms and he soon established himself as a farmer and a gentleman. One of the places he had hired was Stanfield Hall, but ownership was in dispute and the Hall was subsequently physically seized by eighty men and the contents put outside in the rain. The eventual owner was one Thomas Jermy from whom James Rush hired Potash Farm. Thomas Jermy and James Rush had already quarrelled bitterly because James could not keep up his payments on the farm and Thomas had evicted him but had later relented and reinstated him as a tenant. James, however, could not forget the incident and vowed revenge and, if possible, to gain the Hall for himself. He planned the death of Thomas Jermy and then coldly proceeded with his plans.

After having tea with Miss Sandford, James retired to his

bed saying he was feeling too unwell to go to the concert. He had been in the habit of going out at night for a stroll around his woods since poachers had been active, and he intended to catch them. So, at about eight o'clock, he left the house as usual. This time though, in addition to wearing his black cloak, he was disguised by a wig and false side whiskers. Miss Sandford heard him collect his gun before setting out along the road. Turning off along the straw-covered footpath and across the lawn, he hid in the bushes just outside Stanfield Hall. Before long Thomas Jermy came on to the porch at the beginning of his customary constitutional after his evening meal. Fixing Jermy in the sights of his gun James fired and shot him dead.

Racing into the Hall through the side door James was confronted by Thomas's son Isaac who, alarmed by the sound of the shot, was making for the front door. James again lifted his gun and shot young Isaac Jermy dead. Isaac's wife dashed into the hall and, seeing the body of her husband on the floor, screamed for help. Summoned by the call, Eliza Chastney, a servant, rushed in and James Rush, stepping out of the dining-room, fired his gun again and again, hitting Mrs. Jermy in the arm and the servant in the leg.

Before making his escape from the two screaming women James dropped a forged note in the hall which bore the signature of another claimant to Stanfield Hall, thus hoping to lay the blame on someone else.

On reaching his home, James cleaned his gun as quickly as he could, replaced it in the case and went back to his bedroom at about nine o'clock, pausing only to seek out Miss Sandford to tell her how much better he felt after his ten minute walk.

James found it difficult to sleep and who can wonder at that? He got up at half past two and went to Miss Sandford and again reminded her that he had only been out for ten minutes.

His feud with Thomas Jermy was well known and his disguise could not have been good for the two women in the Hall had recognised him. He was arrested by the police the next morning and was committed for trial in the Norwich Spring Assizes. Here he conducted his own defence but his case was hopeless. In the end the evidence against him was overwhelming and a key factor in this prosecution was the evidence of Emily Sandford.

His death by hanging at twelve o'clock on April 21st, 1849, was watched by over 12,000 people, some being brought by train from Yarmouth. He was executed on a scaffold on the bridge over the moat, and the death knell sounded from St. Peter Mancroft Church. Some ten miles away the windows of Stanfield Hall gazed out unblinking and impassively across the April misted meadows as his body hung for an hour, for all to see and remember.

WICKHAMPTON HEARTS

In the ancient church at Wickhampton there is a
stone effigy of Sir William Gerbygge with a lion at
his feet, a flowing tunic over his armour, carrying
a sword and a shield, and, curiously, holding a stone
heart in his hand. His lady in wimple and long robe
is beside him, a loving picture most would say, but
why the heart? That heart has a strange and
macabre story.

During the reign of Edward I around the turn of the
twelfth century, Wickhampton, on the marshes by Breydon
Water, was a place of fine hunting and had one large farm
near the church, whilst the neighbouring village of
Halvergate was rich in arable land. Halvergate was the
better of the two villages by far as it boasted many fine
farms and a noble church.
Sir Valence Gerbygge owned both the villages and he and
his two sons, Gilbert the elder son, and William the
younger son, managed the estate and all who lived on it.
It was a fine estate with farmland rich and good where the
crops thrived. Animal husbandry was profitable, for the
damp pastures yielded lush grazing in the summer and
abundant crops of hay for the cold winter months. There
was ample building material from the timbers in the woods
and the muddy clay from the marshes. Wild life abounded,
making hunting a sporting certainty, and provided cheap
food for the many children. Gilbert and William were
indeed fortunate and the good Sir Valence was forever
telling them so. But they were also quarrelsome and jealous
and Sir Valence often had to reproach them.
Gilbert, being the eldest son, wanted the pride of the
inheritance and his fierce possessive gaze took in all that
was good, and to his brother's, and many of the villagers',
annoyance, he used the word "my" far too much. But
William was not one to take this lightly. He was strong and
his mind was as sharp as a whip. He quarrelled with his
brother incessantly and Sir Valence was at his wit's end to

31

know how to distribute the lands at his death.
But divide them he did, leaving Wickhampton to William
and the better of the two villages, Halvergate, to Gilbert.
He made known his will and prayed for peace as he
breathed his last. But, after his death, there was little
peace. At first William and Gilbert were pleased with their
possessions. They rode around their lands on fine horses
and all was pleasure and gratification. The brothers met
and shook hands and the quiet villagers noted this with a
cynical nod, for they could see the storm clouds gathering.

Next year at ploughing time, when the oxen were yoked in to their ploughs, and the men and women looked forward with gladness to another season, the real trouble started. A field, just north of Wickhampton church, projected far into the boundary of Halvergate, and Gilbert saw this and called to his brother. "That field should be mine", he cried. "It is an obvious mistake, made when the boundaries were drawn." "You already have enough", replied William in a steel-cool voice, "No mistake has been made." But the impetuous Gilbert, angry that he could not sway the younger brother, jumped from his saddle and, running over to William, pulled him from his horse "I will have my way", he shouted, and struck at William with his bare hands. The two brothers then attacked each other with a ferocity that frightened the sturdy country folk who gathered round to watch the fight.

William and Gilbert, unarmed, tore at each other with their bare hands, on the edge of the very field about which they disagreed. They grasped and groped for hair which they could pull out by its roots, ears which they rent, fingers, legs, arms and noses which they scratched, pulled and tore at with unreasoning and inhuman fury. The pent-up differences of all their years were released and they became animals, snarling and viciously snorting, and the villagers watched but dare not intervene.

As the blood began to flow and the fighting became more intense, a demoniac fury gripped the two brothers and they left the world of human recognition. Their finger nails seemed to grow longer, their teeth became fangs, their eyes widened, and the horrified villagers' gazing became a silent and grotesque fascination. The snarls took on a higher note and their fangs and claws tore at each other's throats and breasts. With devilish roars of extreme exulta-tion, William and Gilbert, in a final burst of malice, gripped each other's hearts and tore them out. Lifeless, they lay upon the ground. The awestruck onlookers then saw a divine figure, some said that it was an angel, visit the spot and, to atone for such an inhuman exhibition, turned the

two bodies into stone. In the stone fingers each still
clutched the heart of the other. Silently the brothers were
borne off to their respective churches where the bodies
were laid to rest but, in memory of the brothers' fury and
their shame, the villages were ever afterwards called Hell
Fire Gate (Halvergate) and Wicked Hampton (Wickhampton).

THE HAPPISBURGH SMUGGLER

The church on the cliff top at Happisburgh thrusts its tall tower into the lofty sky over the sea, and tries to bring a saving grace to those who would wrest the spoil from the sea or make journeys over great waters. But, its goodness is needed in the ground at its feet, for just down the hill, a few yards from the tower, is the evil spot of Well Corner.

About two hundred years ago, Sydney Baker came out of Hill House Inn under the church at Happisburgh, well nigh filled to overbrimming with good country ale and lurched down the stony incline on his way home. Having left the soft glow of the candles in the bar, his eyes took little time to adjust to the fitful light of the moon which played hide-and-seek among the scattered clouds. Sydney's frame of mind was calm and happy, the only shadow on it being the thought of his wife the next morning when she would hound him unmercifully for his staying out late. But, the air was warm on that August night in 1800 and Sydney felt good as he rolled past the old well and along the road. What made him turn he did not know: was it the fall of a stone, or the call of an owl? He never knew, but, he turned and then he stood - transfixed - shivering and gasping - unable to move - as a hideous form moved from the direction of the sea and closer, ever closer, to Sydney.
In the clear moments of moonlight he saw it plainly: the figure of a man clutching a sack in his grasp, wearing the clothes of a seafarer. But it was not this that made Sydney afraid. No, it was the fact that the figure glided towards him down the hill because he had no legs ... and because ... as it drew nearer, Sydney could see that the figure's head lay backwards between his shoulders on a horrible strip of skin. Sydney began to gibber as the figure grew closer. But, when the figure reached the well, it dropped the sack down it and jumped in afterwards.
Sydney went hot and cold, but his shaking legs bore him homewards, his eyes starting from his head and his whole

frame articulate with terror. His wife, Thirza, rudely
awakened by the banging of the door and the banging of
furniture began her tirade from her pillow. With lighted
candle she came downstairs, and, seeing Sydney standing
there, continued her fury. Sydney's chattering merely con-
vinced her that he was drunk and she stalked off to bed
taking Sydney with her.

Thirza's feelings were confirmed the next morning when
Sydney would not get up and her aggravation was com-
pounded at 8.30 when Mr. Howes, his employer, came to
find out where Sydney was. He listened to Sydney's tale
with disbelief until the normally sound and sensible Sydney
said that he would not stir from his bed until the mystery
had been solved.

Mr. Howes was puzzled by the change which had been
wrought on Sydney and he spoke of it with three neighbouring farmers that very afternoon when they met to
discuss the harvest. He prevailed on them to wait by the
well with him that very evening. At eleven o'clock they met
and thirty minutes later these four good Norfolk gentlemen
were horror-struck when they all witnessed a further mani-
festation of the apparition that Sydney had seen performing
the self-same actions.

They were as shocked as Sydney had been, but, instead of
seeking bed, though the night was late, they went to Mr.
Howes' home and fortified their spirits with good
'un-excised' brandy! There they animatedly discussed the
night's events and resolved to watch again the next evening.
This they did and again the events repeated themselves,
and again on the third night. By this time Mr. Howes'
brandy was getting low.

Early the next morning Sydney Baker, with three other
men, went to search the well. One man, braver than the
rest, climbed down into the well on a long ladder, and the
others waited at the top. To Sydney's relief, but increased
concern, a body was brought up but with the head and
legs in a sack. Sydney watched with eyes popping out but
was assured by the cool Mr. Howes that 'all would be
settled'.

Later that week Sydney heard on the rural vine, that Mr.
Howes 'knew all about it'. And 'it' turned out to be that the
men who delivered Mr. Howes brandy had quarrelled
amongst themselves about the price of the booty. A man
from Sea Palling, it was, who had met his fate.

Sydney gave up the drink that night and so will anyone else
who lingers too long by Well Corner. For when the moon
is right, the smuggler still glides his eternal way, even
though the old well has been filled in.

WALSINGHAM SHRINE

At Easter and Whitsun especially large number of pilgrims may be seen walking the narrow roads and lanes, as their predecessors of yore did, to the holy shrine of Walsingham. This world-famous focus of pilgrimage is based upon a very strange story.

In the days of long ago, when the good Edward the Confessor, builder of the first Westminster Abbey, ruled the land, there lived in the town of Walsingham a rich young widow named Richeldis de Fervaquere. Her husband, Richeldie, had been the lord of the manor at Walsingham Parva (Little Walsingham) and he had died either in battle or of some illness; the story does not tell us how.
Apparently Richeldis mourned her husband, but did not take his death as an act of punishment from God, for in 1061 she prayed that she might be given a special task to honour Our Blessed Lady, Mary, the mother of Jesus. So fervent was her prayer that Mary appeared to her in a vision and transported Richeldis to Palestine. She was shown the room where the Archangel Gabriel had visited Mary to tell her that she was to be the mother of Jesus. Mary told Richeldis in the vision to make very careful notes of the measurements of the room and then to construct a replica of it in Walsingham. These dimensions Richeldis recorded most faithfully. When she awoke she hardly dared believe her dream, but when it was repeated a second night the air of unreality receded, to be replaced by absolute certainty when she saw the vision again on the third night.
She then made haste to carry out the instructions of her vision and gathered together a fine band of builders and carpenters, and plenty of wood, in preparation for the building. Then it dawned on her that no details of the site had been given, but again this was made known to her in a wonderful way. After a heavy dewfall it was seen that two spaces remained quite dry in a meadow near to a twin of ancient wells, and Richeldis recognised this as a divine

message. Choosing the patch nearest to the wells she measured out the size of the room, 23' 6" by 12' 10", and the builders commenced work.

But nothing went right for the builders. The corner posts would not keep upright, and at the place where one should have been the ground was very rocky; the wood split and it seemed that some evil spell was on the building. The workers threw down their tools and went to Richeldis with stories of their difficulties.

Accordingly she spent the whole night in prayer and in the morning what a sight met their eyes! The wood had been assembled into the room exactly as Mary had told her, but it was on the other dry spot, some two hundred feet further away from the wells. It was accepted by Richeldis and the workmen that Mary and the angels had moved the room to the place where it should be.

After the house was finished, a statue of Mary and Jesus was put into the building and pilgrims came from all over the

world to worship at the place represented by the visions of
Richeldis. Because of the great number of pilgrims, the
road to Walsingham became one of the main highways of
England in the early Middle Ages, and along its route
chapels and inns were built especially to house the pilgrims.
As the Milky Way was said to point the way to England's
Nazareth, it was renamed the Walsingham Way.
Many miraculous cures were said to have been worked by
the waters in the twin wells, and the holy shrine was visited
by young and old, rich and poor, peasants and royalty
coming in their thousands over the five-hundred years of its
life. The last king to visit it was King Henry VIII, who
walked barefoot to the shrine from the slipper chapel.
It was he also who was responsible for the destruction of
the shrine on 18th September, 1534, when Walsingham was
one of the first of the holy places to sign the Act of the
King's Supremacy. In 1537 the sub-prior and ten monks
were cruelly put to death for trying to re-establish the
Priory. Two of them died in the field near the Priory,
which is still called Martyr's Field. The statue of Mary and
Jesus was burnt in Chelsea under the stern gaze of Thomas
Cromwell himself.

In 1931 the chapel was rebuilt by the Rev. Alfred Hope
Patten and has become a centre of pilgrimage once more.

THE OLD DOOR HANDLE

The large iron ring which forms the handle of the disused church in the small village of Southwood between Norwich and Yarmouth is an old sanctuary ring, some people say. But the story told to me has a stránger, but more truthful ring about it.

On the boundary of Southwood there is a large pit, dark and cool. It's side, sometimes shallow, sometimes steep, is overgrown with trees and bushes and an undergrowth that clings to the feet and trips the ankles. It is an ancient pit. Isolated and quiet, Callow Pit could seem an ideal spot for courting couples but it is avoided by the young, and the old still careful of their lives. In the winter its' bottom is covered by a pool of water which vanishes in the early summer sunshine to lie dry but cool in the hot days of August. There is a firm conviction in its neighbourhood that at the bottom of the pit, buried deep in the mud of centuries, is an iron chest which contains a large quantity of gold. But the guardian of the chest fills any would-be treasure seeker, or even wanderer, with dread and alarm. Once upon a time, or so the story goes, two local men, Walter Burton and Bob Pointer talked about the story of the hoard of gold at the bottom of Callow Pit. Times were hard and the scant wages they scraped from their jobs, Walter as a rat-catcher, and Bob as a travelling carpenter, made life for themselves and their families a miserable existence indeed. Walter had a rather shifty look upon his sharp features, but this was more due to the scantiness of his evening meal than from any dishonesty in his nature. His quest for the rat had lent him a certain cunning though and there was envy in his thoughts that could not find ample fulfilment in his work. He and his terrier, Scat, knew the hedgerows well, and the lofty barns and cobwebbed stables of the village were a second home to them.
It was whilst he was eating his meal of bread and cheese that he first struck up a real acquaintance with Bob Pointer, who had been hired to mend the roof timbers in the bullock

41

shed at Southwood Hall Farm. In the fitful April sunshine they sat and ate, talking of the village. Callow Pit and its treasure were discussed and Bob's open-faced humour made light of the danger of trying to get the chest of treasure for themselves. Walter broached the suggestion that they should go searching for the treasure and Bob said that they should go that very night for the moon was rich and full and would give them light.

And so they went, Bob carrying on his shoulder a long ladder he had borrowed from the farm, and Walter a big pole with a hook on the end that he used to haul rats' nests from their holes, and to pull sacks down from tall rafters. Scat snuffled in the undergrowth loving the night's expedition.

The two men made their way to Callow Pit and laid the ladder over it. Clambering cautiously and nervously out along the ladder, they shivered slightly in the damp, eerie, spooky, chilliness. They poked in the mud with the pole and drew up several branches and an iron bar before hooking on to what they thought was a rock, its weight practically immovable. By dint of great effort, the two men wrestled silently with the weight, and the ladder wobbled violently with their exertions. Then, with a splash, the object broke surface and Walter and Bob saw in the silent moonlight that at the end of their pole was an old chest.

Feverishly they hauled the chest up to the level of the creaking ladder, and, having grasped the chest, Bob cried out, "Ah, we have the chest, and even old Nick himself cannot get it from us."

But, he had broken the silence that is essential to success in dealing with either demons or fairies, and instantly the pit was engulfed in a thick acrid vapour and a large black hand, that of Old Nick himself, grasped the chest and a fierce struggle ensued. Scat raced home as though the devil himself was chasing him. Walter and Bob firmly held the pole which passed through a ring on the old chest whilst the ladder lurched violently in the throes of the fight. At last, with a horrible tearing sound, the ring parted from the chest; the treasure fell back into the pit and sunk and the two dumbfounded men still grasped the pole, unable to believe their experience.

They finally pulled themselves together and muttered frightened curses as they dashed off home bearing the ring as a token of the truth of their experience. They may have been deprived of the gold, but they came in for much free beer to unloose their tongues about their adventures in the months that followed.

As a remembrance, the ring was attached to the handle of the village church - a sure token of the truth of the treasure and the evil strength of its guardian.

THE PEDLAR OF SWAFFHAM

On the ends of the pew just before the altar in Swaffham Church are carved the effigies of John Chapman and his dog. These figures are repeated on an old desk in the chancel, while in blue and purple glass in the aisle is yet another portrayal of John Chapman but this time with his wife. His commemoration is due to the story of how he gained his wealth and rebuilt the north aisle of the church in the fifteenth century.

In the hubbub, the noise, the colour, and the mob of people who made up Norwich Market place in the 1440's, John Chapman of Swaffham had his occasional stand. Amid the pedlars with their brooches of amethyst and garnets, bone combs and burnished silver mirrors, serfs with their eggs and furmage, dark skinned men who sold spices such as cloves, sweet canelle and cubebs, jars of mustard from Lombardy, and loaves of wastel bread, stood John, a true Chapman with his copper pots and chargeurs. He had set out early from Swaffham with his packhorse loaded with wares and at the end of the day he had to pack his unsold items, find a beer and lodging for the night before making for home the next morning. It was far too dangerous to be out on the road at night.

He had a long, tiring walk home and after seeing to his horse and merchandise, he went indoors into his small house on the outskirts of Swaffham. He had his meal, all the while complaining to his wife about the shortage of money, and, as the evening was well spent, his tiredness led him to bed where he lay that night in a deep but restless sleep. For he had a vivid dream of a man repeatedly telling him that if he stood on London Bridge he would hear something that would lead to his fortune. So graphic was his dream that he could not forget it. All the next day, and the next, it remained uppermost on his mind, and he could not forget it, try as he would. And, as the hours went by, his conviction led to a growing compulsion to go to London.

His wife's scornful annoyance did not disturb the faith he now felt in the truth of his dream.

So, after a week's preparation, he set out for London with only his dog, and his pack of clothes and food on his back, much to the worry of his poor wife who was sore perplexed by the strange workings of her husband's mind.

After many days travel John arrived in the bustle of fifteenth century London. Finding London Bridge, he took up his station at the end of the bridge and watched the passersby with intent and interested eyes. Some people asked his business and talked with him but he heard nothing that would lead to his fortune. For three days he watched and waited but the passing hours did not shake his assurance.

Then, on the third day, a man asked him why he stood there. So open and frank was his face that John Chapman told him that it was because of a dream. It turned out that the stranger was also a dreamer but one who had no faith in his dreams for he replied, "Alas my friend, if I believed in dreams, I would be as much a fool as you. Recently I dreamed that if I went to the home of John Chapman, a pedlar who lives in Swaffham in Norfolk, and dug under a tree which grows at the back of his house, I would find a buried pot of treasure." Scarcely waiting to thank the man and hardly able to believe his ears John went home as quickly as he could.

On reaching his house, he got a spade and dug furiously, with his wife watching in unbelieving amazement. Eventually he found a box with a curious Latin inscription on the lid. Opening the box with trembling hands, he found it filled with money. Great was his joy, and that of his wife, but the words on the lid of the box worried him. To find out the meaning the crafty pedlar put the box in his window, and some young men who knew the language translated the couplet into:

> Under me doth lie
> Another much richer than I.

So again John Chapman dug, this time deeper than before, and he found a huge pot brimming over with coins and jewels.

His fortune made, and the peace of his mind restored, much to his good wife's relief, the pedlar became one of the members of the gentry of Swaffham. To thank God for his good fortune, he paid for the rebuilding of the north aisle of the church and, to thank John Chapman for his generosity, the good people of Swaffham wove him forever into the patchwork of their town's history.

And there he remains, an emblem for the town, as the sign for Swaffham shows.

BAWBURGH WELLS

St. Walstan, the patron saint of agricultural workers, was born and buried in Bawburgh near Norwich. Even today, traces can be seen of the slipper chapel on a farm, and the shrine in the church. Additionally, there are wells in the neighbourhood which have been wonderfully curative in many instances. A pretty village on the River Yare, Bawburgh has a story that will make old and wise heads wonder and younger ones amaze.

Long, long ago, before the Normans came, the manor house at Bawburgh was owned by a wealthy couple, Benedict and St. Blide, who were related to the royal family. Between the years 960 and 970 they had a son, Walstan, who grew up to love the farm but was also a good scholar. He learned to read, no common thing in those days, and spent hours in his father's library.
Benedict hoped that he would become a great scholar and encouraged his son in every way that he could.
But things turned out very differently from the way that Benedict had planned because, instead of becoming a scholar, Walstan became a farmer and a saint, for he chose to work the land and study the ways of God.
At the age of fourteen, Walstan greatly distressed the good Benedict and St. Blide by announcing over dinner one day that he intended to renounce his family, his learning and his inheritance and seek to serve God and the poor. This disturbed his parents but, true to his word, he changed into his old clothes after breakfast the next morning and walked out of his home and away up the road. His tearful mother had wished him goodbye but expected to see him back after his youthful enthusiasm was spent. He had asked his parents' forgiveness and had tried to leave them peacefully. He walked five miles to Taverham where he met a farmer who was in need of help on his farm. As was the custom of the time, Walstan made a life-long agreement with the farmer to serve him as he wished.

From that day Walstan adopted the life of the farm labourer, working long hours doing tedious hard work on the land, using primitive tools and oxen. He loved the work, finding a quiet but satisfying communion with the life of the crops and the animals, and deriving joy from the slow passing of the changing seasons. He enjoyed meeting the few travellers who passed by on the road, hearing their news and telling them of his own life and faith in the power and love of God. He had few opportunities to give to or to serve others as he was so poor himself. But, one day, a poor traveller came along the road, limping badly on his sore and unshod feet. Walstan, on seeing the plight of the man, shared his simple meal with him and insisted that the traveller take his own shoes.

So annoyed was the farmer's wife when he got home that evening, because Walstan had given his shoes away, that she sent him out to hoe the vegetable plot before giving him his supper. It should have taken two or three hours, but within half-an-hour Walstan had finished and had done the work well. In fact, so well and quickly was the work done that the farmer's wife was dumbfounded by this wonderful act and asked Walstan's forgiveness.

After he had served at the farm for many years the farmer gave Walstan a cart and the produce of a cow in calf. The cow produced two fine young bulls which Walstan trained to draw his cart. They became a great joy in his old age. It is said that on 27th May, 1016 Walstan was visited by God and was told that he had only three more days on earth. Walstan's last wish was that he should be placed in his oxen cart and should be buried wherever it was that they finally came to rest.

He died whilst working on a field in Taverham and there a spring of pure water welled so that he might have the sacrament of the last rites. The farmer placed Walstan's body reverently on his cart and the oxen set forth. Their journey took them through Costessy where they paused in the woods. A second spring of water gushed forth there and this continued to give water until the end of the eighteenth century. The oxen finally stoppd at Bawburgh, his birthplace and final resting place, and it is said that they passed

49

through the north wall of the church. A third spring appeared there and it is to this spring that many miracles were ascribed. The body of Walstan was buried in the north end of the church and a shrine was established over his body.

Visiting the church now, the traveller can see traces of the shrine in the wall of the church and the well is still there, although on private ground.

THE LEGEND OF SHRIEKING PIT

Just off the winding main road running along-side the poppied North Norfolk coast, about two miles inland from Cromer, lies the small village of Northrepps, untouched by time. Find the village shop and the public house, "The Foundry Arms" and then proceed up Hungry Hill towards Sidestrand. Halfway up the hill a sandy lane on the right leads to a grey-green willow-hung pit so deep that it once swallowed a horse and cart with no trace. This is Shrieking Pit.

Tall, graceful and willowy, with long, dark brown hair, soft round face and an evenness of feature and form, Esmerelda was the beauty of the village in 1782. This was her eighteenth year and she blossomed from an attractive country girl into a young maid with all the grace and dignity of a highborn lady. Daughter of a farmworker who lived along Craft Lane, some said that her real father was a guest at the hall where her mother was a serving girl, but this was not so.

Many a young lad dreamed of Esmerelda; many a bold young swain advanced his suit; many a hopeful young boy sought for closer acquaintance - all seeking to inspire her mysterious smile which began with a curve in her tender sensitive lips before it lit two stars in her sparkling dark brown eyes. But Esmerelda also dreamed, and she dreamed of a shifty worthless young farmer from Roughton. He was already married, but, typical of his sort, he merely desired further affirmation of his self-supposed charm and a complement for his own self-fancied good looks. He encouraged her adoration although he knew full well that he could never honour their relationship nor make her life settled and secure. But, full of quiet, contained longing, she forgot tomorrow, thriving in this illicit affair, and seemingly doomed herself to the fruits of passion.

Life in those days held constraints that cannot be imagined nowadays. The young farmer was persuaded to end the affair by the landowner and the rector who threatened to restrict his livelihood if he did not play the faithful husband. Lacking the courage to face Esmerelda he just stayed away, leaving her to weep and sigh in private. Maintaining her cool demeanour she continued her life as a tied housemaid in Shrublands, the farmhouse at the end of Craft Lane. But inwardly her love gnawed at her vital life strings and her elemental longings gradually rose to such a pitch that they could not be contained in sanity.

She had lately taken to lone night wanderings and her favourite walk was along Craft Lane and thence by Sandy Lane to Hungry Hill and so home again. On these night excursions her tortured mind seemed to find relief in the physical exertions, but solitude distils unrequited passion into such a blinding spirit that even basic instincts are disregarded.

One night, one cold night, when a white full moon shone, and the silver world was irridescent in un-natural blacks and whites, Esmerelda moved along Sandy Lane and moaned in a wild will-o-the-wisp manner. She passed a large open pit, its waters steely hard in the moonlight, and her wild spirit stood on the bank and gazed upon its surface. Was it a ripple? Was it a shadow? What evil spirit held the night? What did the poor half-crazed girl think she saw in the water? Was it the image of her lover's face? Without further thought she jumped into the water to join her lover; and, not until she jumped into the waiting water did reason come flooding back. As she felt its chilly embrace, she screamed a wild shriek that echoed in the hills and wakened dogs and people secure in their cottage beds. The second wail brought heads to windows while some shivered in fearful sheets. They knew that something awful had happened and, as the third scream shivered into a shriek which ended sharply, the legend of Shrieking Pit was born.

Some say that on February 24th at midnight something can be heard and seen near the pit; I would not know for nothing would induce me to find out. Even on the sunniest day, the place is cool.

ST. EDMUND

Memorials to St. Edmund abound in Norfolk in the form of dedicated churches, names of villages and local legends. The fact that he lived is beyond dispute, but the strange story of St. Edmund has puzzled historians for years and tested the religious beliefs of many.

It was in the violent days of England's Dark Ages that Edmund was the King of East Anglia, one of seven divisions of the country. He was the son of the King of Saxony and his birth had been foretold in the vision of a Roman Soothsayer.

King Offa of East Anglia, having no son, went on a pilgrimage to the Holy Land to ask for a son, but on the way he visited his relative the King of Saxony and it is fortunate that he did. Here he met and was impressed by the young Edmund and gave him a gold ring signifying that he was the heir to the throne of East Anglia. On the way back from his pilgrimage King Offa died in the Dardanelles and his followers collected Edmund and brought him back to England. They landed at Hunstanton where twelve springs gushed forth to mark the occasion. A chapel was built on the spot and remains of it may be seen near the lighthouse. Edmund was taken to Attleborough where he was trained for kingship and also learnt the Psalter by heart. He had only been there for a year when he was taken to Bures (later Bury St. Edmunds) where he was crowned king by Bishop Humbert of Elmham, on Christmas Day 855. The reason for his coronation was that the Danes were attacking and raiding the coast and a leader was needed to repel the invaders. This he did successfully and for ten years there was peace in East Anglia and Edmund's fame as a just King grew.

Among those early invaders that King Edmund repelled were the Danish soldiers led by their King Lodebroc, who died in the battle. Lodebroc's two sons, Hingwar and Ubba waited ten years, during which time they strengthened

54

and retrained their army, before coming over to East Anglia to wreak vengeance upon the good King Edmund. They landed and marched inland and met King Edmund and his army in battle near Thetford. A great and terrible battle was fought leaving the grass red with the blood from both sides. Great was the slaughter but in the end the Danes routed the army of King Edmund. Among the survivors was King Edmund who escaped but was grief stricken by the slaughter of his subjects. But the Danes were hot on his trail and pursued him relentlessly. He was besieged in a castle near South Buckenham with some of his soldiers, and to escape he merely rode out of the gates. The Danes asked if he knew where King Edmund was, and he replied that he was in the castle when he was, which of course was quite true. The Danes dashed in to the castle only to find it empty. At Hoxne near Dereham he was hiding under a bridge when the reflection of his spurs was seen in the water by a bridal party. They betrayed him to the Danes and he was caught. To this day a stream in Hoxne is called Goldbrook; there is a plaque on the outside of the church showing King Edmund under a bridge; there is even a bridge over which local tradition decrees that no bridal couple should pass.

Having been captured by the Danes, Edmund was taken to a nearby oak tree and tied to it. He was offered his freedom if he renounced his Christian faith and became

the slave of Hingwar, but these things he would not do. So he was used for target practice by the Danes with their bows and arrows, not to kill him but to cause him suffering. After again offering Edmund his life for the same sacrifices, and with his repeated refusal, Hingwar eventually ordered his men to cut off King Edmund's head. This they did, throwing his head into the bushes.

This might be thought to be the end of the story of King Edmund, but far from it. Hingwar himself lived on but he could not shake off his remorse for killing Edmund in such a cruel way and he too became a Christian.

But even this is not the end, for the fantastic stories of the body of King Edmund go on. They tell of his head calling out and being buried near the body in a shrine built near the spot of his death. This is hard to believe but so also are the stories of the cures of all manner of diseases suffered by those who visited the shrine. Stranger still are the stories of how the body would not decay and of how it was exhumed and a monk was put in charge of guarding the body. One of his duties was to cut the nails and hair of the 'dead man'. By the year 955, the head had rejoined the body, only a thin red line showing where the head had originally been severed. The body itself was touted around as a relic and it was thought to have eventually reached Toulouse in the fifteenth century. From there a skeleton was brought back to England in 1901 lying now at Arundel, but the skull is still in Toulouse.

A puzzling tale indeed.

THE BABES IN THE WOOD

The town of Watton, in the south west of Norfolk, stands near an ancient forest, once much larger, called Wayland Wood. On the town sign of Watton are pictured the figures of two children and a robin. Locally the forest is called Wailing Wood - and dialect alone does not account for this - it bears a sad story.

Once upon a time Edmund de Grey lived in Griston Hall a fine house surrounded by rich farmland. He lived with his wife Elizabeth and his two young children Jane and Thomas and they were a happy and good family, well loved by all who knew them. Edmund was a good employer and the men who worked for him served him willingly and well. Elizabeth too was a good house keeper and all the house servants followed her kind and capable instructions. She would have no nurse for the children as she wanted them to know the love of a mother.

And so summers shone and winters passed on this happy family as they lived their good lives in this beautiful corner of Norfolk.

But one August, Edmund and Elizabeth de Grey caught a dreadful illness and they were kept in bed by anxious and caring servants who whispered to the children to stay away from the sick room. Jane and Thomas huddled on the stairs listening to the worried murmurs of the servants as they descended the steps, and their fears were heightened by the strange smell of burning herbs and other potions which were carried upstairs to ward off the risks of infection and to effect a cure. Their anxiety was increased when their feared uncle Robert came to Griston Hall and went up to the room where the sick couple lay. Following him they listened outside the door as the gravely ill father asked his brother to care for the children. In the event of their father's death, Thomas was to inherit three hundred pounds per year and Jane was to receive a dowry of two hundred pounds on her wedding day. If the children died before they came of age, the uncle, Robert, was to inherit

everything. The children heard the uncle vow to keep the
last wish of Edward. "May God never prosper me and mine
if I do not care for your children well, dear brother," he
said.

Both the mother and the father died and Thomas and Jane
were taken, weeping, to the home of the uncle. Life was
much different there, but they settled down, good children
that they were.

But, a year later, the wicked uncle plotted to kill Thomas
and Jane as he was feeling the lack of ready money.
He plotted with two ruffians who were to be paid £50 if
they took the two children into the forest and killed them
there. Telling his wife that the two children were to be
cared for in London, he gave them to the two scoundrels
who led them into the wood. The two children delighted
in the walk and their gay chatter enchanted the two men
who soon wished that they had not accepted the gruesome
task. One of the men wanted to let the children go, but the

other, greedy for the reward, would not relent and a fight ensued. Thomas and Jane quaked with fear as they saw the ferocity of the two men and the fight ended with the merciful man killing the other.

He led the children deeper into the wood and then he told them to wait whilst he went for some food. It was not his intention to return but he did hope that someone else would find them. Tiring of waiting, the two children wandered about eating berries and then they lay down under an oak tree to sleep. They died that night of cold and hunger and in the morning a robin came along and covered their bodies with leaves.

Robert, the wicked uncle, gained the money, but fortune did not smile upon him. His conscience continually reminded him of his crime, his crops did not ripen, his cattle died and his barns burned down. His two sons died on a voyage to Portugal and Robert had to sell his lands to pay his debts and he went to the debtors' prison in Norwich where he died in misery.

The more merciful man, who had abandoned Thomas and Jane to their fate, was caught for another crime and sentenced to death. Before his execution he confessed the part that he had played in the death of the Babes in the Wood, and thus yet another story was added to the history of Norfolk.

AMY ROBSART

Somewhere in Rainthorpe Hall lies the answer to a mystery that has remained unsolved for over four hundred years, and has caused a restless spirit to wander and search. It is all the result of a web woven by Elizabeth I, her favourite and favoured courtier Robert Dudley, and an unwitting Norfolk girl caught up in their connivings.

Amy Robsart, the beautiful offspring of Sir John Robsart of Syderstone, was seventeen years old and already a widow. She was married to Roger Appleyard who had been Lord of the manor at Bracon Ash, Rainthorpe and Stanfield. Life in the spring of 1549 held a promise and delight that made her eyes look forward to tomorrow with a calm and bubbling anticipation. Her parents were wealthy, she was lovely, and she and her step brother, John, in the sheltered byways of Norfolk, knew that life was good. They lived most of their days at Stanfield Hall and, although they travelled little and few travellers came their way, the incidents of the early Middle Ages did not pass them by.

Amy surveyed with interested eyes the efforts of the peasants on her father's estate to better their lot. She felt sorry for them, but knew that it was right for them to accept the benefits and the disadvantages of their station. When the Kett brothers led the local revolution, Amy was shocked by the outrage. She saw as literal knights in shining armour, the soldiers from London who came to quell the Peasants' Revolt as it came to be called. The soldiers stayed in Wymondham, and were led by the Earl of Dudley who set up his headquarters close to Stanfield Hall. Amy got to know the Earl of Dudley and his son Robert very well. So well in fact that a year after the revolution was put down Amy married Robert Dudley in London at a sumptuous wedding attended by the nobility of the land, including the young king, Edward VI.

For some time Amy lived a rich and romantic life, visiting the various houses on the huge Dudley estates all over the country. Their fortunes changed however, when King Edward VI died and Robert's father plotted to place Lady Jane Seymour on the throne. As a reward for his unsuccessful attempt, Robert's father was beheaded, all the Dudley possessions were confiscated, and Robert himself was imprisoned in the Tower. Amy, the loyal and faithful wife, visited Robert regularly, treading the grim, foreboding, dark passageways and stairs of the grey tower.

Great was her delight when he was released after a short time and they came back to Amy's home in Norfolk. There now began a golden period in her life as Robert managed the estates and Amy saw to the households she knew and loved. Her step-brother John lived at Rainthorpe Hall while she spent most of her time at Stanfield, and they became very close at this time.

But Robert aspired to greater things and when Elizabeth I ascended the throne, Robert paid her court, regained his lands, and became the confidante and special envoy of the Virgin Queen. He spent less and less time with Amy and tongues all over the country wagged with tales of 'the king to be'.

Poor Amy was bereft. She had fallen deeply in love with Robert and missed him terribly. She pined and mourned her lost husband and this soon took a toll on her health. She grew thin and her complexion acquired sallow, pale shadows. It was rumoured that she had a tumour, that she was slowly being poisoned, and that soon she would die. She was away from her Norfolk home, and John Appleyard, her step-brother, grew increasingly concerned as to Amy's welfare.

So, he was horrified, but not over-surprised when news of her death on September 8th 1560 came to Rainthorpe Hall. It appeared that she had fallen down the stairs at Cumnor Hall in Berkshire in somewhat suspicious circumstances. It could have been an accident for Amy was in a weak state, and descent of the tall stairs in those ancestral halls was not free from danger. It could have been murder for it was well known that Robert wanted to be rid of Amy and there is also some evidence that even Elizabeth I might have been involved. The third possibility was that Amy

committed suicide for she despaired of her husband's infidelity and may have felt that the unknowingness of death was preferable to the loneliness of separation. Or she might have taken her life hoping that the scandal would embarrass Robert and Elizabeth so that they could never be married.

John Appleyard openly swore that it was murder and was so indiscreet in his assertions that he was put into prison and only released when he apologised and stated that he agreed with the jury's verdict that it was an accident.

On the evenings of September 8th the ghosts of John Appleyard and Amy Robsart meet and whisper on the lawn at Rainthorpe Hall. If someone could eavesdrop on their conversation, it could solve the mystery of that unfortunate lady who died such a tragic death. But take care, for vengeance is in the air.